Original title:
Whispers of the Pothos

Copyright © 2025 Creative Arts Management OÜ
All rights reserved.

Author: Lucas Harrington
ISBN HARDBACK: 978-1-80581-734-5
ISBN PAPERBACK: 978-1-80581-261-6
ISBN EBOOK: 978-1-80581-734-5

Beneath the Veil of Vines

In the corner, she peeks out,
With a grin and a pout.
Hiding secrets of the room,
Dancing tall; it's pure bloom.

Lurking low with a cheeky sway,
Turning leaves in disarray.
A playful spirit, bold and bright,
In a leafy, green delight.

Hidden Stories in Each Leaf

Each leaf has a tale, oh so great,
Of kitchen spills and dinner plates.
Tales of toast, and crumbs galore,
Stories told behind the door.

Gossip flows through every vine,
A leafy laugh that feels divine.
Eavesdropping on all the fun,
This plant's got stories, one by one.

The Lullaby of Climbing Greens

Up the wall, they twirl and twist,
Singing soft songs, how can you resist?
A melody of green, a gentle tease,
Filling the air with giggles and ease.

In the light, they sway and play,
Bouncing jokes throughout the day.
A concert of green, so sprightly,
The room's alive, oh so brightly.

Intimacy Among the Shadows

In corners dark, they find their class,
Whispering secrets as they pass.
A joke exchanged with a wink and sway,
Life's too short for a serious day.

Creeping close, in leafy disguise,
Tickling thoughts and quirky sighs.
In the shadows, laughter blooms,
In nature's art, joy resumes.

In the Embrace of Nature's Breath

In a pot, the leaves do sway,
Sipping sun in a silly way.
Roots beneath do wiggle, twist,
Chasing bugs that dare resist.

A tangle here, a tangle there,
They plot their world with utmost flair.
"Who needs space?" they giggle loud,
As they form a leafy crowd.

Harmonies of Leaf and Light

Photosynthesis, a clever trick,
Leaves composing tunes so quick.
With every sip of morning dew,
They sing a song for me and you.

In the sun, they dance and prance,
Green performers in a leaf-filled trance.
"Please don't pluck me, I'm no snack!"
They warn with a dramatic flap.

Plant Dreams and Silent Seasons

Underneath, they dream of fame,
Aspiring vines, they play the game.
"Next spring, we'll climb this wall!" they cheer,
Throwing shade and growing near.

Seasons change, their visions grow,
"Let's throw a party!" they all crow.
But come the frost, they'll bundle tight,
Wishing for a sunny night.

The Subtle Dance of Roots

Roots underground, a secret ball,
Twirling, swirling, having a ball.
"Watch your toes!" one whispers loud,
As they jostle underneath the crowd.

They twist and turn with joyful pride,
A hidden dance that none can ride.
"Invisible ink," one rootsy chap grins,
"Bringing joy where the fun begins!"

Soft Nestle of Leaves

In a corner where sunlight peeks,
A plant giggles, in green it speaks.
A leaf tickles a nearby cat,
Who jumps high, looking quite flat!

It sways with a mischievous sway,
Making the dust bunnies play.
A spider, who silently weaves,
Wonders what mischief it believes!

Embrace of the Green Veil

Underneath the leafy shroud,
A gnome sneezes, it's quite loud.
The pot's too warm, he takes a seat,
But a mushroom makes him retreat!

Around the vines, gossip takes flight,
"Did you see the snail's new height?"
Giggles echo, a light mist,
As ferns shake, they're hard to resist!

The Secret Lives of Plant Spirits

In the night, the spirits convene,
Designing plans for a raucous scene.
They throw a party, plants in a row,
Dancing to tunes from below!

Cacti prickle with a witty jest,
While daisies compete, who can jest best.
All the orchids flaunt their flair,
Reminding everyone, 'It's the style we wear!'

Dappled Dreams Among the Greens

In dappled light, the leaves conspire,
To spread a rumor, oh what a fire!
"Did you hear the fern's latest fling?
With the lily? Oh! That's quite a thing!"

The ivy rolls its leafy eyes,
While the succulents plan a surprise.
Together they laugh, sipping dew,
Saying, "Who knew plants could be so cool too!"

Beyond the Green Facade

In the jungle, vines grow tall,
They hide all secrets, one and all.
A squirrel once tried to climb so high,
He got stuck, much to my surprise!

Leaves whisper tales that make me chuckle,
Of wandering insects and their shuffle.
A lizard struts with all its flair,
While the frogs compete for who can stare!

A monkey swings from branch to branch,
Terrified of a near cat's ranch.
But leaves just shake and root chortles,
As creatures play in leafy portals.

So if you hear a giggle near,
It's just the plants, have no fear!
Jungle life is a funny show,
With laughs and antics only it knows!

The Hidden Heart of the Jungle

In the jungle deep, a riddle lies,
Where maybe a parrot will tell no lies.
A turtle slow, thought it was fast,
But found himself stuck in the grass!

A jaguar once wore a flowered crown,
Claiming to be the best-looking around.
But when he tripped, oh what a sight,
He rolled downhill, took quite a flight!

A wise old tree with a trunk so wide,
Said, "Come on over, let's take a ride!"
Its branches cracked jokes about the breeze,
While the monkeys laughed with utmost ease!

Jungle tales, they tickle the mind,
With critters and plants that are one of a kind.
So listen close, and you just might hear,
The punchlines spoken from creatures near!

Tender Tendrils of Truth

Tendrils twist like gossip vines,
Spreading rumors of feasting times.
A snail claims it can outrun the sun,
But everyone knows it's just for fun!

A vine braids tales of nighttime chats,
Between bats who wear their pointy hats.
While critters debate who jumps the best,
The spider's web stays out of the jest!

Lizards gossip about a new leaf,
Claiming it's the jungle's best motif.
Yet when the rain falls all around,
Their fashion sense just can't be found!

So join the plants on their silly spree,
Where laughter grows on every tree.
Tender tales and jests unfurl,
In this lively, leafy, wrinkled whirl!

Luminous Hues of Solitude

In shades of green, where silence plays,
Lies a creature who brightens days.
A firefly claims it lights the way,
But flickers out, "hey, I'm on a holiday!"

The ferns laugh softly, with secrets shared,
Of tales unmapped and moments bared.
While in shadows, the moss gleefully speaks,
Of ancient trees with cheeky peaks!

Under the glow of an emerald hue,
A tortoise tells tales that seem too true.
"I've traveled far, through muck and mire,
Only to find this little quagmire!"

So if you stroll through this vibrant place,
You might just smile, or see a face.
In solitude, where wild things play,
Luminous giggles light the way!

Shadows of Tender Soliloquies

In a pot of green delight,
Leaves have gossip, oh so light.
They sway and twist, with glee they dance,
In their own little leafy romance.

A squirrel stopped by for afternoon tea,
Critiquing foliage, just like me.
He said, 'This fella needs some care!'
While I chuckled, without a care.

The plant next door has quite the flair,
It's wearing the sun like fancy hair.
While I examine my own little sprout,
It rolls its eyes, as if to pout.

So here's a toast to green confessions,
In secret shade, we share obsessions.
If only they could share a laugh,
Those leaves might write their own green staff!

The Embrace of Climbing Sentiments

Tangled vines amidst the wall,
Don't mind the cat's heroic fall.
They stretch and reach for heights unknown,
While I sit here with my cone.

They whisper sweet nothings to the breeze,
And tease the sunlight with such ease.
I overheard a leaf declare,
'We need a vacation – anywhere!'

The trellis laughs, a trusty friend,
Supporting dreams 'round every bend.
But all these plants, so full of schemes,
Could use some grounding in their dreams.

So let them climb, let them play,
As I sip my tea and sway.
What a life, this garden spree,
With all their wild camaraderie!

Gentle Curves of Botanical Confessions

In the corner sits a shy fern,
With secrets that it won't discern.
It curls up tight, a nervous mess,
While others flaunt their leafy dress.

Oh, dear cactus, standing proud,
Making it awkward, like a crowd.
"Don't touch, I'm sharp!" it seems to say,
Yet craves some love in its prickly way.

The herbs nearby share saucy tales,
Of daring growth beyond the scales.
"Mint's got sass," the basil chimes,
While I record their funny rhymes.

As petals giggle in the sun,
They sprout rebellion, just for fun.
A garden's world of cheeky cheers,
With antics echoing through the years!

The Muted Poetry of Growing Minds

In quiet corners, thoughts take flight,
As seedlings ponder day and night.
"Why do the humans look so frazzled?"
Oh, dear little sprout, we are all puzzled.

A daisies' daydream, quite profound,
Wonders where the sun is bound.
"Maybe it's hiding?" it muses aloud,
In the gentle sway of a curious crowd.

The herbs join in with witty tales,
Of garden games and treasure trails.
"Let's seek the sun, oh what a plan!"
But all they find is the soggy pan.

So here we giggle, green and spry,
With nature's whispers gently nigh.
In laughter woven through the leaves,
We'll grow together, as nature weaves!

The Embrace of Dappled Light

In the corner, a leafy friend,
Hiding secrets that never end.
A dance of shadows, twirls and bends,
With a cheeky grin, the sunlight sends.

Every leaf a cheeky smile,
Snickering softly, 'Stay for a while!'
Though rooted firm, it dreams of flight,
Oh, how it loves the dappled light!

Tiny tendrils, like fingers, creep,
Towards the books that never sleep.
"Focus!" I say, but it just beams,
While plotting its garden-themed schemes.

With every sip of morning dew,
It cackles, "More fun than a zoo!"
In this green kingdom, laughter glows,
Where every quirk of nature shows.

Sonnet of Winding Vines

A spiral journey, oh what a thrill,
This twisty vine knows how to chill.
With a little wiggle and a hop,
It scales the shelf, refusing to stop.

"Fetch me snacks!" it slyly implies,
Just as I roll my weary eyes.
Each curl a joke, a playful tease,
As it wiggles right behind the cheese.

"Not the fridge!" I mock in despair,
Yet there it clings, without a care.
It dreams of heights, of mixer blades,
In this leafy realm, mischief never fades.

So here's to you, my playful sprout,
With every twist, you make me shout.
When life gets dull, just climb and sway,
Your winding ways brighten my day.

Threads of Green Lullaby

A gentle rustle, a leafy tune,
As vines frolic in the afternoon.
They sing of adventures, carefree and bold,
In shades of green, their tales unfold.

A sleepy blossom, eyes heavy as bricks,
Dreams of spaghetti, oh what a mix!
"Twirly vines," it hums, "let's dance tonight,"
While a curious cat prepares for a fight.

With every bend, the laughter grows,
In the garden where silliness flows.
"Join us now!" the leaves all cheer,
As they stretch their arms and disappear.

In this world of green giggles and cheer,
Every moment brings friends ever near.
So let's sway with a little glee,
In this melody of family tree.

The Soft Secret of Growth

In the darkest corner, a secret lies,
A sprout that dreams of reaching the skies.
With a gentle nudge and a sly grin,
It plots its way to the sun, my kin.

"Not quite ready to face the day!"
It whispers low, then shimmies away.
Bursting forth with a flair so strong,
In this leafy kingdom, you can't go wrong.

"Watch me grow!" it sings with glee,
A leafy rocket, can't you see?
With a wiggle, a dance, and a twirl,
This sprout just dreams of the grandest whirl.

Yet patience, dear friend, is part of the game,
In the garden of giggles, we all feel the same.
So let's nurture this joy, let it burst forth bright,
With a hint of silly, under the moonlight.

Quiet Murmurs of Nature

In the garden, giggles bloom,
A cactus wearing a funky costume.
The daisies gossip, they can't keep still,
As squirrels steal acorns, what a thrill!

The roses blush in the sunlight's tease,
While bees buzz in a dance, if you please.
The grasshoppers leap with a skip and hop,
Making all the flowers giggle non-stop.

Sighs of the Heart's Foliage

A vine complained of a dreadful shoe,
Too tight, too bright, it just couldn't do.
It sighed of dreams of a leafy ball,
Where ferns could wear crowns, standing tall.

The old oak chuckled, roots in a twist,
As acorns debated who'd make the best list.
The ivy winked and rolled its green eyes,
And all the branches shimmied, oh my!

Dances of the Lush Tendrils

Tendrils twirled in the summer air,
With sun hats made of petals, oh so rare.
They slipped and slid on the garden floor,
Chasing butterflies, giggling more.

A merry band of leaves took the stage,
Their rustling laughter was all the rage.
As raindrops joined in, a raucous tune,
Nature's own circus, beneath the moon.

A Symphony of Subtle Green

In the orchestra, leaves play a tune,
With a berry's giggle, under the moon.
The cucumbers played their sly little part,
While pumpkins rolled in, with joy in their heart.

A soft breeze chimed in with a peppy beat,
As grass excitedly tapped its tiny feet.
Roots rumbled together, a comical sound,
In this garden hall, laughter knows no bound.

Gossamer Threads of Nature's Voice

In the garden, leaves do dance,
Tickling air, they take their chance.
They gossip softly, oh what fun,
Secret tales of sun and run.

Vines wrapped tight in a silly hug,
Who knew plants could feel so snug?
Twirling tales with every breeze,
Nature's jesters among the trees.

Stealing sunlight, don't you dare,
The photosynthesis affair!
They giggle under the sky so blue,
Leaves waving as if to say 'boo!'

With every rustle, laughter roars,
Nature's antics, who needs shores?
Swaying roots in a silent game,
Watch them prance—they're kinda tame!

The Quiet Symphony of Growth

In dark corners, roots creep slow,
Singing tunes that only plants know.
A leafy orchestra starts to play,
Grassy notes in a bright array.

Creeping tendrils, a string quartet,
Strumming fingers, let's not forget.
Each leaf nods to the funky beat,
Soil's percussion—oh, what a treat!

With raindrops tapping like a drum,
The whole space fills with a soft hum.
Photos rippling in a dance,
Every shift, a romancing chance.

Nature's laughter, serene and bright,
As worms wiggle in pure delight.
A comical show as roots entwine,
In this odd ballet, all are fine!

Emblem of Serene Connectivity

A fern and vine decide to chat,
Spreading joy—imagine that!
Branches wave like hands in glee,
In leafy circles, wild and free.

Their silent talks are grand and bold,
Stories of sunshine and pure gold.
Twisted tales of garden fame,
Well-connected, but none to blame.

With every nudge, a secret's sprouted,
Tendrils reach where roots have crowded.
Branches high, they play their role,
Hiding laughter, deep in the soul.

In quiet corners, they conspire,
Debating who has the best attire.
Vines in laughter, leaves aghast,
Nature's play—it's a charming blast!

Whispers in the Canopy

In the treetops, mischief brews,
Leaves sharing gossip, old and new.
A squirrel pauses, ear to the bark,
    Curious tales ignite a spark.

Acorns falling like jokes on the ground,
Mischievous winds swirl all around.
They plot in shadows, a leafy scheme,
    Life's a party—a verdant dream!

From branches, swings the chattering crew,
    Bouncing jokes like morning dew.
    Every rustle, a giggle shared,
Buds drummin' beats, none ensnared.

Among the leaves, humor reigns tall,
Nature's jesters—pick up the call!
With laughter stitched in every vein,
    In the canopy, joy will remain!

Intertwined Whispers of Life

In the corner sat a vine,
With leaves that playfully entwine.
I told it jokes, it laughed right back,
But still, it never lost a leaf on track.

A spider swung from thread so thin,
Said, "Hey, that plant's a local win!"
As I poured water, it made a splash,
Then sent me off, saying, "Make it fast!"

The sunbeam danced upon the floor,
While the plant whispered, "Give me more!"
My dog peeked in, oh what a sight,
A vine with flair, a true delight!

So here we sit, both green and spry,
I cracked a grin, the leaves replied.
With laughter shared in leafy lines,
This joyful plant's now part of mine.

The Gentle Sound of Flourishing

In the sunlight, leaves do sway,
Dancing lightly through the day.
A gnome nearby, oh, what a tease,
Declared the leaves were such a breeze!

A squirrel scampered up the stem,
Declaring himself a flourishing gem.
"These leaves are mine!" he seated tight,
"I'm reigning here; it feels just right!"

The whispering greens, a funny tune,
Swayed along with a silver spoon.
While the cat sneezed, a startled leap,
Chasing shadows where secrets sleep.

And when night crept with soft delight,
The plants giggled, feeling light.
In this garden where laughter blooms,
Nature's joy fills all the rooms.

Embracing Nature's Stories

In the garden, tales unfold,
Of leafy legends never told.
A flower winked, a rosebud beamed,
"Join our saga!" – how they dreamed.

The leafy tales are full of cheer,
Each rustle soft, it called me near.
A snail chimed in, "I take my time,
But even I think this is prime!"

A ladybug flew with a flair,
"You think your roots could use some air?"
As petals giggled in the breeze,
A dance began, oh what a tease!

With insects boasting tales so bright,
They shared their stories in the night.
These plants, they chortled, held their grace,
In nature's heart, our funny place.

In the Quiet of the Leafy Realm

In quiet corners, stories bloom,
Among the leaves, there's much to room.
A beetle claimed a leafy seat,
Said, "I'm royalty — isn't that neat?"

While a worm sang in soft refrain,
"This leafy spot, oh what a gain!"
Frogs croaked in, with humor galore,
Echoes dancing off every floor.

The moon peeked in, a curious sight,
As plants whispered secrets of delight.
Caterpillars chewed munchy greens,
In fits of laughter, they formed teams!

And thus in this leafy realm so fine,
Nature giggled, entwined with time.
With beetles, frogs, and plants so sly,
In this green domain, oh my, oh my!

The Language of Climbing Souls

In a jungle full of vines so sly,
The leaves hold secrets, oh me, oh my!
They tell us tales when no one's around,
Of all the mischief hidden and found.

A chameleon smiles, tongue flicks in glee,
Offering gossip from the tall, green spree.
With whispers so loud, yet silent as night,
These climbing souls giggle, what a delight!

Nature's Unvoiced Epistles.

The ferns seem to chuckle, tucked in their beds,
While daisies roll laughter inside their heads.
Swaying so lightly, they share their delight,
Of how squirrels jump, always ready to bite.

Beneath swaying branches, the rabbits engage,
Drafting plans for a mischievous stage.
"Let's hop like we mean it!" they giggle and cheer,
As the sounds of the forest draw closer, my dear!

Secrets in the Shadows

In the shadows, where mischief may brew,
A caterpillar pens all the funny things too.
"Did you see that snail? Oh, what a slow show!"
The mushrooms erupt with a spontaneous glow.

With each little giggle, the secrets conspire,
A rabbit in glasses, reads tales by the fire.
The fireflies wink, with each blink a tease,
As the night air fills with chuckles and ease.

Lush Echoes Beneath the Canopy

Beneath the great canopy, vines dance in pride,
Tickling each other, they giggle and glide.
The crickets compose a very loud tune,
While frogs in the mud hold a dance party soon.

Nature's orchestra plays all the right notes,
With grasshoppers clapping and toads in their coats.
Laughter erupts from the roots and the leaves,
In this green world where humor believes!

Echoed Secrets of the Forest

In tangled greens, the squirrels plot,
With acorn hats, they twist and trot.
A raccoon giggles, eyes so wide,
While mossy stones provide a guide.

The owls hoot gossip, soft and sly,
As shadows dance and breezes sigh.
A leaf drops lightly, causing fits,
Frogs leap and croak with silly bits.

The trees exchange their leafy views,
In secret notes, they share the news.
Twirling branches hold their breath,
While nature plays a game of chess.

Beneath the ferns, a rabbit schemes,
To bake a cake from forest dreams.
With mushrooms spry, it stirs the pot,
While giggling grubs munch on the lot.

Tender Touches of Green Life

An ivy vine takes a cheeky climb,
Tickling toes in a race against time.
With sunny smiles and shadows long,
A daisy croons a playful song.

A cactus wears a party hat,
While ladybugs dance on a mat.
The daisies join, in full array,
Swaying like they're on parade all day.

In the garden, a worm does the twist,
While dandelions shake a fist.
Beneath a bloom, a snail takes a break,
With dreams of butter in a leafy flake.

The sun winks down with a beam of cheer,
As flowers laugh, the coast is clear.
Nature's humor, bright and spry,
In the petal's secret lullabies.

The Art of Silent Growth

A tiny sprout in stealthy cheer,
Wonders how it grew without a peer.
It stretches wide and yawns so deep,
While beetles giggle in their sleep.

Roots exchange their quiet lore,
Sneaking snacks from what's in store.
With inching vines, they race for fun,
A tangled game beneath the sun.

The mushrooms have a secret fight,
For who can glow the most at night.
While grasses whisper tales so sly,
Of who's the tallest, and who's awry.

Amidst the ferns, a lizard struts,
With a top hat on, it's oh so nuts.
Nature's jesters in leafy clothes,
Celebrate growth in its silent prose.

Enigmatic Trails of Nature

In nature's maze, the paths unwind,
With shortcuts taken, laughs are blind.
A hedgehog dons its spiky wear,
As butterflies float without a care.

The trails twist like a silly dance,
Each turn a chance for a laugh or chance.
With every step, a secret found,
While chipmunks chatter without a sound.

On mossy rocks, the ants parade,
Formations wild as if they played.
While crickets chirp a funky beat,
And stretch their legs on tiny feet.

In full bloom, they point and jest,
A hidden world, a leafy fest.
With every rustle, jokes unfold,
In trails of greenery, stories told.

Mystical Muses of the Green

In a pot sat a sage, quite grand,
With thoughts of the world, all unplanned.
He tuned in to leaves, quite alive,
Gossiping tales that helped him thrive.

With vines that twist, they dance and sway,
A party of greens, come what may.
"Did you hear what the fern just said?"
"No, but I dreamt of a mossy bed!"

They chuckle and giggle, a leafy crew,
Plotting adventures from morning dew.
In bright sunny spots, they raise a toast,
To moments of laughter they love the most!

As shadows grow long, they settle down,
A chorus of cacti wearing a crown.
"We're the wise ones of this splendid scene,"
They chime in unison, all sharp and green!

Eyes of the Leafy Canopy

High above, the leaves all squint,
Peering down like they've got a hint.
"Look at that human, tryin' to climb!"
"His balance is worse than a monkey's rhyme!"

The sunlight flickers, beams playing tag,
While squirrelly acrobats dance like a hag.
"Oh dear, here comes trouble, grab the nuts!"
"Hide in the branches, avoid the ruts!"

Laughter erupts from the leafy crew,
As they plot a prank on the gardener too.
"Let's swap the pots, what's he gonna say?"
"Probably thank us for the new display!"

Giggling softly, in shades of green,
The canopy watches the silly scene.
Each rustling leaf shares tales of their days,
In a world of absurd, delightful ways.

The Intimate Threads of Growth

Tangled in gossip, the roots did weave,
Plotting a scheme, should they deceive?
"Let's pull him in, that sleepy old frog!"
"Or at least convince him to dance on a log!"

With every sprout, a plan made anew,
Adventures of dirt and a curvy view.
"What's that? A worm with dreams of the sky?"
"Let's tell him tales as he wiggles by!"

They huddle close, sharing sunlight's grace,
Plotting their journeys in leafy embrace.
"We're the rulers of soil, can't you see?"
"And soon enough, we'll grow into a tree!"

With roots intertwined, they burst into song,
A symphony of laughter, it won't be long.
For every tiny leaf knows how to cheer,
In this green kingdom, there's nothing to fear!

Embraces in the Shade

Under a shelter of leaves, cozy and tight,
Laughter erupts, a comical sight.
"Pass the nectar, let's raise a cheer!"
"But watch your aim, oh dear, here comes a deer!"

The ferns flip their fronds, rolling with glee,
As they dodge a dandelion who's sailing free.
"Careful with that, it might give you sass!"
"I'd rather wear flowers, what a classy pass!"

Cacti chuckle at the soft, leafy crowd,
"We thrive in the sun, but we're way too proud!"
"When it rains, we'll all trade our best jokes,"
"Let's see who cracks first, our favorite folks!"

Shadows play games with soft summer light,
In this garden of giggles, everything's right.
Together they dance, so happy and bold,
In cuddly cool spots, their laughter unfolds.

Subtle Hues of Heartfelt Thoughts

In the corner, green and spry,
Creeping gently, oh my, oh my!
It seems to listen, never judge,
With every twist, it gives a nudge.

Plant or friend? It's hard to tell,
With leafy charms, it casts a spell.
I talk to it of dreams and snacks,
It nods along, no silly quacks!

I bless the day it came to stay,
And brightened up my gloomy way.
With funny shapes that curve and sway,
I'm convinced it's plotting play by play!

By morning light, it tends to creep,
Encouraging my thoughts to leap.
Is it friendly, or just a tease?
Oh dear plant, do you aim to please?

Murmurs in the Hanging Garden

A leafy friend above my head,
Who drips with gossip, or so it's said.
I glance up high, it giggles low,
Sharing tales from the plant life show.

"Bugs are in, but I am out!"
It whispers sweetly, without a doubt.
"On sunny days, we dance and spread,
While you just sit, your book ahead!"

With tendrils stretching, it often sways,
Mocking my routines, in fun-filled ways.
Every pothole of boredom, it fills,
While laughing at my lack of thrills.

A greenish sage, with much to say,
Its laughter spills at the end of day.
In the hanging garden, love's confide,
A funny chat with a leafy guide!

Lullabies of Verdant Dreams

Dreams float softly on leafy beds,
Where cozy plants weave silken threads.
They hum to me a leafy tune,
In the quiet light of the glowing moon.

"Don't fret, dear friend, don't lose your way,
Join our leafy cabaret!"
With laughter rich, they sway and dance,
While I just ponder my next chance.

The breeze tickles as I softly snore,
While leaves jive and spirits soar.
Tiny donuts of dew drop grace,
While green companions set the pace.

With every twitch, they craft a jest,
In the realm of leaves, I am a guest.
So let's embrace the fun and dream,
For life's a funny leafy theme!

Unspoken Bonds Beneath the Soil

Deep beneath, where secrets weave,
The roots exchange, much to believe.
In the dark, they crack a joke,
While the plants above play cloak and poke.

"Did you hear what the daffodils said?"
"Only that your leaves are quite in the red!"
Beneath the soil, their bonds are tight,
Sharing laughter throughout the night.

My little green pals giggle away,
As I revel in their nightly play.
Each day they poke their heads out wide,
To tease the sun, with joy and pride.

Unseen humor in the darkened ground,
In laughter's cradle, joy is found.
While I sip tea and write my notes,
My leafy friends share what time promotes!

Heartbeats Among the Foliage

In the garden where giggles chime,
Leaves tap dance to a secret rhyme.
A squirrel in shades, quite the flair,
Steals all the snacks without a care.

The daisies gossip, heads held high,
While butterflies swoosh through the sky.
A hidden frog croaks a tune of cheer,
As the nearby snail says, "I'll take a year!"

Each plant sways with a playful nudge,
While shadows flirt, none will judge.
Laughter bubbles like dew at dawn,
In this patch where liveliness is drawn.

As sunbeams winkle in playful jest,
Nature joins in a silly fest.
Who knew foliage could be so fun?
With each heartbeat, the laughter's spun!

Shadowed Reveries in Bloom

Amidst the leaves, a secret pact,
The roses tease, oh how they act!
A turtle jokes, 'I'm winning the race!'
While dandelions blow, in a whirling chase.

The vines conspiring with whispers loud,
Chunky bugs flaunt, but no one's cowed.
Under the shade, a party brews,
With berries sharing the juiciest clues.

A winking leaf twirls in delight,
Chasing shadows, playing hide and sight.
The irises snicker with vibrant hues,
While daisies giggle, sipping the dews.

When the moon peeks with a silver smile,
The garden's antics stretch for a while.
Each bloom has tales, that's surely true,
In this tricky place where giggles accrue.

The Secret Song of Nature

Fog on the grass sings melodious tunes,
A frog hops jiving to the swell of the moons.
The trees sway gently, a comedic dance,
While whispers play tricks in nature's expanse.

Bees buzzing jokes as they sip from bloom,
A critter parade emerges from gloom.
Silly ants march while the blossoms beam,
In this garden of giggles, life's a dream.

A petal drops down, sends the grass in fits,
As wind swoons by, creating small hits.
Laughter erupts; they can't help but sing,
In this vibrant realm where joy takes wing.

With each rustle, a chuckle's bestowed,
Nature's the comedian, sharing the road.
So we join in this grand, funny throng,
To celebrate life with a playful song!

Green Sighs of Affection

In the pot, where the vines twist and twirl,
A gnome drops in with a hat in a whirl.
Cactus chimes in with a prickly grin,
While the leaves are snickering, 'Let's begin!'

The soil laughs deep, harboring secrets,
While tiny seeds aspire with their regrets.
'Grow up fast!' the ivy shouts with glee,
As potted herbs sip their herbal tea.

A lizard sunbathes, soaking the rays,
While the ferns debate the best viney ways.
'Forget the weeds!' the daisies propose,
With petals in colors that nobody knows.

Through all these shenanigans happening here,
Nature flutters with joy and good cheer.
In the garden's heart, under sparkling skies,
Laughter blooms on the greenest sighs!

Soft Murmurs in the Understory

In the shadows the vines play,
Giggling leaves whisper all day.
They tickle the toes of the ground,
Chasing critters all around.

A squirrel rolled over in glee,
He jumped on a leaf, oh so free!
'Is that lunch or a prank?' he thought,
As the vines curled, a game they sought.

The earthworms pretended to dance,
Making everyone join in the prance.
The sun peeped down, so surprised,
At the fun that nature devised.

But don't tell the gardener, dear,
Or he'll come chase you, never fear!
With a trowel and gloves in the sun,
He'll laugh with the leaves, oh what fun!

Hidden Dreams of the Climbing Vine

A vine dreams of whimsical heights,
Plotting grand plans for silly delights.
Can you see it, climbing so high?
With a leaf scarf waving goodbye!

'Well, up to the roof, here I go!'
Cried the stretch of green with a glow.
But a crow cawed loud, 'What a sight!'
As it tangled in twigs, oh what a plight!

The cat on the fence tilted his head,
Thinking, 'That vine needs a new thread.'
With a purr and a wink, he replied,
'Just swing to the left, take it in stride!'

And down came the laughter of blooms,
As the cat showed the vine how to zoom.
Together they made quite the pair,
Creating a racket, laughter in air!

The Allure of Nature's Confessions

Nature speaks in secret tones,
With every rustle, it groans and moans.
The flowers gossip, petals all bright,
'What's the latest? Did you hear last night?'

A daisy danced, saying, 'I'm in!'
'Have you seen that bug, a real win?'
Their chatter flows like a river's song,
'These tales of ours can't be wrong!'

The bushes hummed a playful tune,
Embarrassed to sing 'neath the full moon.
They whispered secrets, oh what a scene,
'This garden's a party, so fresh and green!'

And as the sun rose, laughter still spun,
The petals shouted, 'Isn't this fun?'
Each leaf and twig shared a chuckle,
Making the wild world happily snuggle!

Clandestine Chants from the Canopy

Up high where the canopy twirls,
The leaves are plotting with giggly swirls.
'Come dance with us, swing to the breeze,'
'Together we'll giggle, aim to please!'

A parrot squawked, 'Oh such a clatter!'
As branches twisted in ridiculous chatter.
The monkeys swung, laughing away,
Playing tag with the fronds in the fray.

Amid the roots, a hidden shout,
'What's that noise?' a curious sprout.
'Oh, it's just nature wanting a show,'
As the canopy put on its best glow!

With the critters all joining the spree,
The trees sang loud, 'So wild and free!'
And in the hush of the twilight's gleam,
They formed a ruckus—a leafy dream!

The Soliloquy of Leafy Souls

In sunlit corners, greens conspire,
To plot a dance on winds of fire.
One leaf insists it's quite the star,
While others giggle from afar.

Vines twist and curl, an acrobatic show,
"I can swing higher!" shouts Joe the Joe.
With silent laughs, they dangle low,
As plants, they know just how to flow.

The cactus rolls its beady eyes,
"Don't touch my spines! I'm full of lies."
While ferns whisper back with glee,
"Who needs a prick when you can be free?"

So here in this patch, laughter blooms,
In leafy tales and sunny rooms.
Nature's jesters, green and bold,
Turning silence to stories told.

Chains of Green Whispers

On chains of green, they twist and sway,
Each leaf has something weird to say.
"Did you hear what Fern got up to?
She donned a hat made of bamboo!"

As rubber plants roll their eyes with glee,
"I'll bet they're scheming; haven't you seen?"
"Hold my leaf!" shouts one with flair,
"Time for some wild pranks; we dare!"

In the quiet garden, laughter stirs,
Where petunias gossip and poke fun at hers.
"Did you smell that? No, not the dirt!
It's just Daisy's new perfume, quite a flirt!"

Tales of shenanigans on sunny days,
In vines and petals, fun displays.
Nature's drama, in pots and trays,
A green comedy in blooming arrays.

A Garden's Silent Soliloquy

In the garden, a whisper floats,
Of curious blooms and leafy coats.
"Shall we host a party, dear Thorn?"
"Just text the daisies to adorn!"

A squirrel walks by, a curious sight,
He snickers at flowers, pure delight.
"Those daffodils think they can dance,
But I've seen better moves at a glance!"

The busy bees buzz with a tune,
While lilies giggle, shaking at noon.
"Bring out the nectar! Let's have a feast,
Our garden's alive; it's a wild beast!"

With petals waving, the sun takes a bow,
As roots tap dance, a lively row.
In this silent play, humor reigns,
Where nature laughs and joy remains.

The Subtle Art of Nature's Lullaby

In the gentle sway of leafy tales,
A chorus of giggles in breezy gales.
"Why did the cactus join a band?
To show off his prickly new hand!"

Each leaf a jest, a clever wink,
"I'd rather be dead than drink that stink!"
Said the basil, rolling with laughter,
"To be part of that stew? Disaster!"

The sunflowers stretch with pride so bright,
"Sunshine is my only spotlight!"
Meanwhile, violets blush in charm,
"I'm just here to keep it warm!"

So in this world of green delight,
The lullabies bloom under soft moonlight.
Nature chuckles in subtle ways,
Crafting joy in its leafy plays.

The Soft Caress of Nature's Palette

In the garden, plants gossip tight,
With leaves that dance in morning light.
A tomato grins, all ripe and red,
While basil tries to style its head.

The daisies chuckle, a cheerful troupe,
As the worms wiggle in a little loop.
The sunbeams poke from cloudy places,
While shadows strike a pose with graces.

When raindrops prance on windowpanes,
The flowers hum some catchy refrains.
A dandelion wearing a golden crown,
Blows fluff and giggles, "I won't back down!"

In this vivid world, the colors play,
Each hue a laugh, brightening the day.
Nature's palette, a comedy spree,
Reminds us all, to let laughter be.

Beneath the Veil of Time

Beneath the layers of leafy dreams,
The clock ticks slow, or so it seems.
A bumblebee buzzes, lost in thought,
While lily pads hold secrets, or so they ought.

The roots are plotting a tiny coup,
As squirrels laugh, joining the queue.
The stones on the path wear quirky hats,
While frogs debate the best of spats.

Time curls up in a sunlit nook,
Joking silently, with each little crook.
A creeping vine wraps around the past,
While petals giggle, "Let's hold fast!"

The whispers of seasons blend and sway,
As nature throws its fun soirée.
With each tick, the adventures unfold,
In the garden of laughter, life's pure gold.

The Hidden Pulse of Green

Under the soil, the secrets hum,
Where beetles dance, they beat the drum.
A tangled web of giggles and glee,
Every wriggly worm a jokester, you see.

In vines that climb, a riddle plays,
As ivy whispers its leafy ways.
The ferns tease the sunlight with glee,
"Catch me if you can!" they chant with glee.

The vibrant brush of emerald hues,
Turns the mundane into a news.
With every flutter, fronds start to spin,
In the chaos, laughter's where we begin.

With roots entwined, they share their jest,
In a world where green is the best.
Nature's heartbeat, full of cheer,
Pulling us close, drawing us near.

Delicate Movements in the Stillness

The breeze tiptoes through quiet leaves,
Carrying secrets that nature weaves.
A ladybug laughs as it rolls on by,
While wise old trees exchange a sly sigh.

In the stillness, life isn't quite calm,
As petals flutter, spreading their charm.
A chipmunk juggles acorns with flair,
While the crickets chirp, unaware of the stare.

A spider's web catches the light just right,
Glistening brightly, a sparkling sight.
With every giggle from the boughs above,
The world spins tenderly, wrapped in love.

In nature's dance, all is in sync,
With moments of chuckles, on the brink.
As we stand by, with curious grins,
We join the dance where the fun begins!

The Unseen Dialogue

In shadows green, they chatter low,
Leaves gossiping, a leafy show.
"Did you see that?" one leaf did tease,
"That branch over there looks like a sneeze!"

Their laughter sways in the lightest air,
While roots below just sit and stare.
"Don't let the gardener hear our tales,"
Said vine to vine, as their giggle sails.

One spoke of bugs that hid and danced,
Another chimed in, slightly entranced.
"I think I saw a squirrel with flair,"
"Nonsense! He's just a fluff of hair!"

The sun dips down, their voices blend,
As branches bow, they twist and bend.
With every rustle, they share their glee,
An unseen jest, in their leafy spree.

Green Secrets in the Breeze

A leaf invited a breeze to play,
"Do you know the gossip from yesterday?"
The breeze just chuckled, swirled around,
"Those petals think they're quite profound!"

Tall stalks leaned close, hanging on tight,
"Tell us more! This cheeky delight!"
A flower blushed, its color bright,
"I heard a rumor that night is light!"

The grass nearby grew wild in jest,
"Well, I'm the softest, I'm clearly the best!"
Roots in a tangle, most wild of all,
"Just hold your ground, we'll have a ball!"

The evening whispered on zealously,
As the greens gathered most eagerly.
They took to giggles, a verdant spree,
In the warm embrace of a rustling spree.

The Subtle Art of Intertwining

Two vines met, a spark ignited,
"Do you think our dance is quite one-sided?"
With twists and turns, they joined the game,
"You lead and I'll follow, how fun, how tame!"

A slight entangle, a gentle tug,
"Oh dear, am I snug or just a bug?"
Laughter echoed through the tangled knot,
"We're the life of the party, whether we like it or not!"

A frond chimed in, with a playful grin,
"You're no match for how I spin!"
"Is that so? Well, catch me if you dare,"
The vines entwined, without a care!

Their laughter rang through the leafy halls,
As ferns waved up, and petals sprawled.
In every knot, a story told,
Of friendship rich and bonds of gold.

Hushed Cadence of Flora

In the garden's heart, they shared a jive,
"Can you believe we're all alive?"
A daisy winked, a rose did sigh,
"Just look at us, oh me, oh my!"

Petals fluffed, wings flitted about,
"We have such fun, without a doubt!"
"Here's a secret, do not tell,
I think the moon fell under our spell!"

Chirps from crickets, echoed the night,
As clovers giggled in sheer delight.
"Shh! The gardener's on his way!"
Whispered the leaves, in a hushed ballet.

Yet, as he passed, they all held tight,
For nothing brewed under starlit light.
Together they danced in the cool night air,
In a hush of laughter, their secrets laid bare.

The Language Only Leaves Understand

In the breeze, they giggle and sway,
Tickling the branches, come what may.
A rustle, a shuffle, the gossip's begun,
Who knew that leaves could have so much fun?

The sunbeams dance on chlorophyll skin,
While friendly buds share a chuckle or grin.
"I saw that bird—what a clumsy flight!"
The leaves burst with laughter, it's a joyful sight.

In the shade, they weave hilarious tales,
Of mischief and frolic in soft, playful gales.
The critters join in, for they've got the knack,
When branches start joking, there's no holding back!

So next time you stroll beneath leafy attire,
Listen close, they're adding to the choir.
Nature's comedians, with a soft little tease,
The language of leaves is a giggle-filled breeze.

Nature's Quiet Soliloquy

In the forest, the trees hold a secret so dear,
A solo performance, that all want to hear.
With a creak and a crack, they tell their own tale,
Of squirrels and shadows, and how to entail.

One trunk giggles softly, while others nod fast,
"Did you see that snail? It was quite the blast!"
With branches that wave and bark full of glee,
It's nature's top comedy, waiting for thee.

From daisies to oaks, they join in the jest,
With whispers that echo, they're truly the best.
The breeze carries chuckles through leaves green and grand,
A laughter-filled soliloquy, hand in hand.

So take a deep breath, let the giggles surround,
For nature's own soliloquy is merry and sound.
In the heart of the woods, it's an amusing spree,
Where silence is funny, oh just wait and see!

The Enigma of Green Shadows

Beneath the trees, a riddle does bloom,
The shadows are plotting, making room.
What's that rustle? A mischievous fox?
Or just Boris the beetle, eyeing his socks?

The shadows play tricks, they dance and they sway,
As if they are saying, "Come out and play!"
With giggles that echo through twilight's embrace,
In the enigma of green, there's always a race.

"Did you hear that wind? It's whispering jokes!"
Said the wispy young leaves, shaking like folks.
"Why did the twig cross the path with such flair?
To dodge all the squirrels, they're nuts, I declare!"

So amidst all this laughter, the shadows conspire,
While fireflies twinkle, igniting desire.
In the mystery of green, there's fun to be found,
With secrets and giggles the trees welcome loud.

Boughs of Breath

Up high in the boughs, the air's filled with cheer,
As branches share stories that all want to hear.
The leaves rustle softly, like giggles in air,
Creating a symphony, both joyful and rare.

With roots deep in laughter, they sway with delight,
The twigs tease the breeze every day and night.
"What's green and has leaves that shake like a dancer?
A tree with a joke! Come, take a chancer!"

In each gentle sigh, the trees share a tale,
Of critters and breezes that swiftly set sail.
The boughs all are breathing, with giggles as air,
Turning tiny troubles into a light-hearted flair.

So when you look up at the foliage high,
Remember they're laughing, just give a try.
Nature's big theater, where humor's the plea,
In the boughs of breath, all is fun-loving glee!

Shadows of Nature's Embrace

In the garden's green parade,
Leaves doing a wiggly charade.
Frogs leap in a sprightly dance,
While ants in tuxedos take their chance.

Bugs boast of their nightly feats,
While squirrels nod to tasty treats.
Nature claims it's all so grand,
As roots plot with a hushed command.

Vines drape like a comical shawl,
Tickling the blooms, making them sprawl.
The sun winks in its golden attire,
While the clouds riff like a choir.

And when twilight steals the show,
The critters gather for a glow.
In shadows, laughter takes a stand,
Nature's antics, all so unplanned.

Whispers of the Wild

In the trees, secrets take a stroll,
As raccoons practice their rock and roll.
Owls might hoot with a playful grin,
Challenging each other, who'll win?

Squirrels argue over acorn fare,
While crickets play tunes without a care.
The breeze teases with a gentle tickle,
As flowers giggle, oh what a pickle!

Bumblebees buzz in a dizzy whirl,
While fireflies light up the night with a twirl.
Nature's laughter echoes wide,
As critters always seem to collide.

With each rustle, the wild takes the lead,
Creating stories of nature's misdeed.
From bushes thick to skies untamed,
Every whimsy in wildness, unframed.

Life in the Thicket

In thickets thick with clever wit,
Nature's juxtapositions fit.
With hedgehogs donning spiky crowns,
And rabbits bouncing with their frowns.

A ladybug, in a top hat flies,
While bugs make bets on who can rise.
The flowers grumble at the vine,
As the twigs try to draw the line.

Mice rehearse for a big premiere,
In a world where nobody's sincere.
The owls are critics, wise and spry,
Making notes as time passes by.

And sunlight pings around like glee,
As shadows play, and all agree.
In the thicket, nothing seems normal,
Just laughter and chaos, a wild eternal.

Ties of Tendrils

Tendrils twist in a silly loop,
As the garden throws a wacky scoop.
Vines tangle in a dance divine,
Struggling to fit in a straight line.

The flowers gossip, oh what fun,
About the frogs who can't seem to run.
The sun's rays laugh, scattered and bright,
Shining down on nature's delight.

Lizards lounge in the shade so slick,
Playing cards, they're quite the trick.
The daisies join in for a chat,
While the dandelions prance in a hat.

Ties of tendrils, binding with cheer,
Nature's comedy, oh so dear.
In joyous chaos, life unfolds,
With laughter and glee, the tale is told.

Veils of Verdant Hues

In a room where plants take charge,
A pothos vine thinks it's large.
It sprawls across the ceiling fan,
Claiming space like an eager fan.

Green tendrils dance with delight,
Chasing dust bunnies in flight.
They tickle noses, make you sneeze,
These leafy friends just never freeze.

With every twist, they snag a shoe,
"I'm just trying to help," they coo.
"The more the green, the better the style,"
They fashion jade with a cheeky smile.

And when the sun shines bright and clear,
They plot a scheme to persevere.
"Let's fill this house with leafy cheer,"
As laughter echoes loud and near.

The Language of Leaves

Oh, the secrets that they keep,
With leaves so lush, they never sleep.
They gossip on the windowsill,
Telling tales of a moody chill.

A leaf will curl when cats come near,
And flap around when friends appear.
They laugh and chatter, oh so sly,
While daring squirrels pass by.

If you listen close, you'll hear,
A vine discussing its frontier.
"Have you seen that wall I climbed?
My victory was well-timed!"

These leafy fellows, full of fun,
Plotting mischief in the sun.
Each day a new caper to weave,
In the curious language of leaves.

Serpent's Embrace in Green

In shadows lurks a playful vine,
Pretending it's a python fine.
With twists and turns, it wraps around,
Giving pillows a leafy crown.

"I'm just here for the cozy look,"
The plant insists, like a storybook.
It slithers low, then climbs so high,
"How do you love your plant?" they sigh.

At night it prowls with leafy grace,
Trying to win the cat's old place.
The feline jumps but can't quite see,
The sneaky vine's new victory.

With each embrace, it steals the show,
In the house where green dreams grow.
A plant that thinks it's sly and keen,
Is truly a serpent, proud and green.

Tales of the Climbing Vines

Once I met a plant named Lou,
Who claimed to know what plants can do.
He climbed the shelf and swung about,
Saying, "Life's just one big route!"

With every leaf, he'd tell a tale,
Of jungle hops and windy gales.
"I once saw a bird dance in rain,
And I said, 'Dude, let's do that again!'"

He wrapped around my coffee mug,
Saying, "Chill, I'm just a snug bug."
And with a wiggle, he would tease,
"Just living life with all due ease."

So if you see a vine so bold,
In the corner, green and gold.
Remember Lou, the legend fine,
Who taught us all to climb and shine.

Secrets in the Green Shadows

In the corner of the room, they scheme,
A leafy crew plotting in a dream.
When I water them, they giggle and sway,
Telling tales of the plants on holiday.

Sneaky stems with secrets to share,
Whispering gossip without a care.
Each leaf a storyteller, vibrant and bright,
Spinning yarns under the pale moonlight.

I laugh as they plot their garden heist,
Stealing sunlight, oh, they're so precise!
With tendrils like fingers, they reach up high,
Making plans to wave at the passing fly.

Among the pots, a riotous crowd,
I'll keep their mischief, but quiet, not loud.
For if the sun hears their silly chatter,
We might end up with a plant-based platter!

Tendrils of Silent Conversation

In the jungle of my living room space,
The vines gossip softly, a leafy embrace.
A pothos named Larry gives wisecracks with flair,
While Edna, his mate, just rolls her green hair.

They hang from the ceiling, with such great style,
Telling each other jokes that make them all smile.
If you listen real close, you might just hear
A punchline that's grown without any fear.

Who knew that plants could be such a hoot?
They giggle each time I step on a root.
In their leafy world, no humor is slight,
Their leaves flapping wildly, what a sight!

So every morning when I give them a cheer,
They sway in agreement, "We love having you near!"
With their tendrils entwined, they share a good vibe,
In their funny little world, they all come alive!

Echoes Among the Vines

Under the table, a gathering so loud,
The vines have a party, oh, how they're proud!
With leaves in a twist, they boogie and sway,
Dancing in shadows, a plant cabaret.

They mimic my sneeze, then all start to laugh,
Trying to tickle the pot with a leaf's other half.
'Does it tickle?' I wonder in playful surprise,
Their choruses echo, I can't believe my eyes!

What a ruckus, a riotous plant parade,
Caught with their roots down—the mischief is made!
I swear, their small giggles hide under the fray,
As I pass by, they just start a new play.

Next time you water, just be sure to stay,
As their stories unfold, hip-hopping away.
For among those green tendrils that twist and entwine,
It's a party of laughter that's perfectly fine!

The Language of Leaves

In the jungle of my home, they chatter and cheer,
The leaves speak a language that's crystal clear.
With a rustle and flutter, they share all the facts,
About how to trap flies or where to find snacks.

A corkscrew vine takes the lead in this ball,
Spinning wild stories while they all have a thrall.
With a wink of their tips, they mimic my phone,
Ringing off the hook in their leafy tone!

"Did you hear about that cactus?" they chime,
"He keeps bragging about how he can outshine!"
They whisper and giggle, their shells all aglow,
Plant drama and feud, what a bizarre show!

So here's to the leaves, each one with a quirk,
In their leafy debate, there's such playful work!
As I sit and listen, I start to believe,
This plant life is more than just roots and leaves!

Threads of Conversation in the Air

In the corner, a vine starts to twist,
Chatting with a pot, both can't resist.
A chubby leaf giggles, sways to and fro,
The sun joins in, with a cheeky glow.

Gossipy roots tap dance underground,
Sharing tales of the sights that they've found.
One leaf grumbles, 'I need some more light!'
The other replies, 'Just wait for the night!'

A Tapestry of Green Syllables

Lively leaves drape, a colorful sight,
They murmur softly, no need for a fight.
A curl here, a twist there, creating a scene,
Every shade of green, so proud and so keen.

In the wind, they giggle, a frolicsome crew,
Telling secrets that only they knew.
"Don't be so stiff!" a young sprout cries,
"Bend with the breeze, under bright sunny skies!"

Leaves Turning to Listen

Each leaf turns its face, to catch every word,
Listening close, as the world gets absurd.
A rumor spreads from one branch to another,
"I swear I saw a snail, it was moving like thunder!"

Branches chuckle, swaying with glee,
"Oh, tell us, dear friend, how fast can it be?"
A leaf quips, "Quicker than a cat on the run!"
They erupt into laughter, under the sun!

The Whispering Greenhouse

In a greenhouse packed, where the greens like to rave,
One leaf takes the lead, oh, how bold and brave!
"Let's tell the caterpillars to throw us a party,
With all of our friends, it'll be very hearty!"

The ferns roll their fronds, with a snicker and smirk,
"Just make sure the slugs don't come; they'll lurk!"
Amidst potting soil, they all shed their care,
Dancing to tunes in the warm, humid air!

www.ingramcontent.com/pod-product-compliance
Lightning Source LLC
Chambersburg PA
CBHW072221070526
44585CB00015B/1438